All I want to Do is
Stay in My
Pajamas & Watch
My Favoriete
Hallmark
Holiday Movies
All Day long

My Notes

My Notes

All I want to Do is
Stay in My
Pajamas & Watch
My Favoriete
Hallmark
Holiday Movies
All Day long

My Notes

My Notes

All I want to Do is
Stay in My
Pajamas & Watch
My Favoriete
Hallmark
Holiday Movies
All Day long

My Notes

All I want to Do is
Stay in My
Pajamas & Watch
My Favoriete
Hallmark
Holiday Movies
All Day long

My Notes

My Notes

All I want to Do is
Stay in My
Pajamas & Watch
My Favoriete
Hallmark
Holiday Movies
All Day long

My Notes

My Notes

All I want to Do is
Stay in My
Pajamas & Watch
My Favoriete
Hallmark
Holiday Movies
All Day long

My Notes

My Notes

All I want to Do is
Stay in My
Pajamas & Watch
My Favoriete
Hallmark
Holiday Movies
All Day long

My Notes

My Notes

All I want to Do is
Stay in My
Pajamas & Watch
My Favoriete
Hallmark
Holiday Movies
All Day long

My Notes

My Notes

All I want to Do is Stay in My Pajamas & Watch My Favoriete Hallmark Holiday Movies All Day long

My Notes

My Notes

All I want to Do is
Stay in My
Pajamas & Watch
My Favoriete
Hallmark
Holiday Movies
All Day long

My Notes

My Notes

All I want to Do is
Stay in My
Pajamas & Watch
My Favoriete
Hallmark
Holiday Movies
All Day long

My Notes

All I want to Do is
Stay in My
Pajamas & Watch
My Favoriete
Hallmark
Holiday Movies
All Day long

My Notes

My Notes

All I want to Do is
Stay in My
Pajamas & Watch
My Favoriete
Hallmark
Holiday Movies
All Day long

My Notes

My Notes

All I want to Do is
Stay in My
Pajamas & Watch
My Favoriete
Hallmark
Holiday Movies
All Day long

My Notes

All I want to Do is
Stay in My
Pajamas & Watch
My Favoriete
Hallmark
Holiday Movies
All Day long

My Notes

My Notes

All I want to Do is
Stay in My
Pajamas & Watch
My Favoriete
Hallmark
Holiday Movies
All Day long

My Notes

All I want to Do is
Stay in My
Pajamas & Watch
My Favoriete
Hallmark
Holiday Movies
All Day long

My Notes

My Notes

All I want to Do is
Stay in My
Pajamas & Watch
My Favoriete
Hallmark
Holiday Movies
All Day long

My Notes

My Notes

All I want to Do is
Stay in My
Pajamas & Watch
My Favoriete
Hallmark
Holiday Movies
All Day long

My Notes

My Notes

All I want to Do is
Stay in My
Pajamas & Watch
My Favoriete
Hallmark
Holiday Movies
All Day long

My Notes

My Notes

All I want to Do is
Stay in My
Pajamas & Watch
My Favoriete
Hallmark
Holiday Movies
All Day long

My Notes

My Notes

All I want to Do is
Stay in My
Pajamas & Watch
My Favoriete
Hallmark
Holiday Movies
All Day long

My Notes

My Notes

All I want to Do is
Stay in My
Pajamas & Watch
My Favoriete
Hallmark
Holiday Movies
All Day long

My Notes

All I want to Do is
Stay in My
Pajamas & Watch
My Favoriete
Hallmark
Holiday Movies
All Day long

My Notes

My Notes

All I want to Do is
Stay in My
Pajamas & Watch
My Favoriete
Hallmark
Holiday Movies
All Day long

My Notes

My Notes

All I want to Do is Stay in My Pajamas & Watch My Favoriete Hallmark Holiday Movies All Day long

My Notes

My Notes

All I want to Do is
Stay in My
Pajamas & Watch
My Favoriete
Hallmark
Holiday Movies
All Day long

My Notes

All I want to Do is
Stay in My
Pajamas & Watch
My Favoriete
Hallmark
Holiday Movies
All Day long

My Notes

My Notes

All I want to Do is
Stay in My
Pajamas & Watch
My Favoriete
Hallmark
Holiday Movies
All Day long

My Notes

My Notes

All I want to Do is
Stay in My
Pajamas & Watch
My Favoriete
Hallmark
Holiday Movies
All Day long

My Notes

All I want to Do is
Stay in My
Pajamas & Watch
My Favoriete
Hallmark
Holiday Movies
All Day long

My Notes

My Notes

All I want to Do is
Stay in My
Pajamas & Watch
My Favoriete
Hallmark
Holiday Movies
All Day long

My Notes

All I want to Do is
Stay in My
Pajamas & Watch
My Favoriete
Hallmark
Holiday Movies
All Day long

My Notes

All I want to Do is
Stay in My
Pajamas & Watch
My Favoriete
Hallmark
Holiday Movies
All Day long

My Notes

All I want to Do is Stay in My Pajamas & Watch My Favoriete Hallmark Holiday Movies All Day long

My Notes

My Notes

All I want to Do is
Stay in My
Pajamas & Watch
My Favoriete
Hallmark
Holiday Movies
All Day long

My Notes

My Notes

All I want to Do is
Stay in My
Pajamas & Watch
My Favoriete
Hallmark
Holiday Movies
All Day long

My Notes

All I want to Do is
Stay in My
Pajamas & Watch
My Favoriete
Hallmark
Holiday Movies
All Day long

My Notes

My Notes

All I want to Do is
Stay in My
Pajamas & Watch
My Favoriete
Hallmark
Holiday Movies
All Day long

My Notes

My Notes

All I want to Do is
Stay in My
Pajamas & Watch
My Favorite
Hallmark
Holiday Movies
All Day long

My Notes

My Notes

All I want to Do is
Stay in My
Pajamas & Watch
My Favoriete
Hallmark
Holiday Movies
All Day long

My Notes

My Notes

All I want to Do is
Stay in My
Pajamas & Watch
My Favoriete
Hallmark
Holiday Movies
All Day long

My Notes

My Notes

All I want to Do is
Stay in My
Pajamas & Watch
My Favoriete
Hallmark
Holiday Movies
All Day long

My Notes

All I want to Do is
Stay in My
Pajamas & Watch
My Favoriete
Hallmark
Holiday Movies
All Day long

My Notes

My Notes

All I want to Do is
Stay in My
Pajamas & Watch
My Favoriete
Hallmark
Holiday Movies
All Day long

My Notes

My Notes

All I want to Do is
Stay in My
Pajamas & Watch
My Favoriete
Hallmark
Holiday Movies
All Day long

My Notes

My Notes

All I want to Do is
Stay in My
Pajamas & Watch
My Favoriete
Hallmark
Holiday Movies
All Day long

My Notes

My Notes

All I want to Do is
Stay in My
Pajamas & Watch
My Favoriete
Hallmark
Holiday Movies
All Day long

My Notes

My Notes

All I want to Do is
Stay in My
Pajamas & Watch
My Favoriete
Hallmark
Holiday Movies
All Day long

My Notes

My Notes

All I want to Do is
Stay in My
Pajamas & Watch
My Favoriete
Hallmark
Holiday Movies
All Day long

My Notes

My Notes

All I want to Do is
Stay in My
Pajamas & Watch
My Favoriete
Hallmark
Holiday Movies
All Day long

My Notes

All I want to Do is
Stay in My
Pajamas & Watch
My Favoriete
Hallmark
Holiday Movies
All Day long

My Notes

My Notes

All I want to Do is
Stay in My
Pajamas & Watch
My Favoriete
Hallmark
Holiday Movies
All Day long

My Notes

*All I want to Do is
Stay in My
Pajamas & Watch
My Favoriete
Hallmark
Holiday Movies
All Day long*

My Notes

My Notes

All I want to Do is
Stay in My
Pajamas & Watch
My Favoriete
Hallmark
Holiday Movies
All Day long

My Notes

My Notes

All I want to Do is
Stay in My
Pajamas & Watch
My Favoriete
Hallmark
Holiday Movies
All Day long

My Notes

All I want to Do is
Stay in My
Pajamas & Watch
My Favoriete
Hallmark
Holiday Movies
All Day long

My Notes

My Notes

All I want to Do is
Stay in My
Pajamas & Watch
My Favoriete
Hallmark
Holiday Movies
All Day long

My Notes

My Notes

All I want to Do is Stay in My Pajamas & Watch My Favoriete Hallmark Holiday Movies All Day long

My Notes

_____

_____

_____

_____

_____

_____

_____

_____

_____

_____

_____

_____

_____

_____

_____

_____

_____

_____

My Notes

All I want to Do is
Stay in My
Pajamas & Watch
My Favoriete
Hallmark
Holiday Movies
All Day long

My Notes

All I want to Do is
Stay in My
Pajamas & Watch
My Favoriete
Hallmark
Holiday Movies
All Day long

My Notes